MRS MULROONY'S

FLY-AWAY

FRENCH BLOOMERS

BY THE SAME AUTHOR

Yemen Rediscovered (*Longman*)
Bahrain: Gulf Heritage in Transition (*Longman*)
Syria in View (*Longman*)
Scotland through the Ages (*Michael Joseph*)
London Heritage (*Michael Joseph*)
A Traveller's Companion to the West Country (*Michael Joseph*)
Journeys into Medieval England (*Michael Joseph*)
Ireland through the Ages (*Michael Joseph*)
The Architectural Heritage of Britain & Ireland (*Michael Joseph*)
Victorian Britain (*Weidenfeld & Nicolson*)
New British Architecture in Germany (*Prestel*)
FlipDesigns (*Prestel*)
FlipSigns (*Prestel*)
Off Course (*Lulu*)
Conundrum's Book (*Lulu*)
Dream of a Summer Night (*Lulu*)
Farthing Abbey (*Lulu*)

MRS MULROONY'S

FLY-AWAY

FRENCH BLOOMERS

Michael Jenner

ISBN 978-0-9558480-4-9

For my father who loved to laugh.

A

SIZZLING

TALE

OF

LOVE

SONG

AND

OUTSIZE

UNDERWEAR

Our story begins in a neat terraced house in the east London suburb of Walthamstow.

"A very nice, bright, sunny day in prospect. Any remaining pockets of rain and cloud clearing quickly from the west..."

Today's TV weatherman is not Mrs Mulroony's personal favourite. She prefers the gangling chap, that funny geezer with the teeth and big glasses who waves his arms around like a windmill.

"This will be followed by oodles of sunshine..."

Oodles? The chap doing today's forecast is the other one, a silly little man who grins like a gibbon or some smarmy salesman trying to get his foot in the front door. Most likely his backside on the sofa too. Then perhaps invite himself for a cup of tea, a couple of custard cream cookies, and who knows what next? Doesn't bear thinking about.

"…and a gentle south-westerly pussyfooting in off the Atlantic, nothing too strong, mind you, just a nice breeze to take the edge off the heat."

"Pussyfooting?"

But weather is weather no matter who stands in front of the map. And Mrs Mulroony is no dunce. She peers knowingly at the complex lines and symbols on the wall chart behind the forecaster, appraising them with the eye of a meteorological expert. If only the daft weatherman would get out of the way she could work out the perishing forecast for herself.

"In fact, it looks like a perfect day for hanging out the washing, ladies."

"Ladies? Washing? Bloody cheek! Silly old fool! Like to see him wash his own whatsits."

Mrs Mulroony is more than a little annoyed. She had already come to the conclusion that today would be just right for hanging out the washing. But she is damned if she's going to do it now that talkative twat on the telly has told her to.

However, the washing thought is firmly lodged in her brain. It simply won't go away. She thinks long and hard. After a few minutes deep reflection, Mrs Mulroony manages to remind herself she had the perfect-day-for-hanging-out-the-washing thought all on her tod well before that halfwit stuck his oar in. She now heaves herself out of her comfy armchair and waddles over to the window.

"Looks like it'll stay nice and dry. Perfect day for a spot of washing, I reckon."

A mysterious smile smoulders briefly on Mrs Mulroony's lips, lighting up her face. Not exactly the sort of smile you'd expect from a lady about to do the washing. But right now when Mrs Mulroony thinks washing what she actually has in mind is something special. She is going to wash her recently purchased pair of seriously enormous French knickers.

The actual size cannot be revealed without discourtesy to a lady. So let's just say that they are way off the chart and only available via special mail order. Made of pure white silk they are, with lovely frilly bits along the edges. They have such a sheen she slips into them smooth as a hippo down a water chute. Not that hippos do that sort of thing, mind you. The fancy French bloomers fit her like a glove. They feel light as gossamer, so light she might be wearing no knickers at all, which is quite a thrill in itself.

She'd ordered them from a catalogue, just the one pair to start with. Thought she'd better try them on for size and so on before stocking up. They had arrived last week. It was love at first sight. Mrs Mulroony had never before owned a pair of knickers that fitted her half so well. She sent off immediately for a dozen more but was shocked to discover that the mail order company had gone bust, belly up, out of business. With no clues in the knickers as to where they came from, except for a neatly stitched label with the three words *MADE IN FRANCE*, she realised this might be the only pair she'd ever get her hands on.

France, this was not a lot to go on; and rather perplexing too. For generally speaking Mrs Mulroony didn't have much time for that strange country full of foreigners with their funny accents and garlicky breath, or so she was led to believe. In fact, she'd never got all that close to a real live Frenchman and could hardly understand one word of the lingo.

But when it came to French knickers, that was something else. She supposed you'd want them to be made in France, now wouldn't you? Well, of course you would. The French were masters of the art of *lingerie* which was what they called smalls or underwear. And this particular pair was the *crème de la crème* and her personal pride and joy. They really took *le biscuit*, and owning just the one pair made them even more special. She might never see their like again.

Lovingly, Mrs Mulroony starts to wash her French knickers, kneading them slowly like dough in a deep square old-fashioned sink. She whips up such a frothy lather she soon has soapy suds crawling up to her elbows tickling her soft pink skin in a most pleasurable manner. Then she rinses them under the tap, squeezing out the water between her large hands with a blend of strength and gentleness.

The thought of putting them in the steel jaws of a washing machine or spin dryer is quite unthinkable, even though according to Mrs Mulroony's common sense an unthinkable thought makes no sense at all.

When she is finally done she smoothes them out on a towel before pegging them up on a washing line that hangs in a long loop between the apple tree and a ramshackle shed in her overgrown back garden.

Exhausted from all the effort, Mrs Mulroony goes indoors and slumps down into her comfy armchair. Its creaking wooden frame and squeaking iron springs adjust complainingly to her weight. From this position she gazes fondly through the French windows at her French knickers. She reckons that's quite a lot of France to be having in Walthamstow all at once. But that's the way it is nowadays, isn't it? Everything coming from somewhere else.

Her view from the armchair is as pretty as a postcard. Looking up she watches her French knickers flapping in the sunshine, billowing in the breeze against a lovely background of radiant blue sky and dazzling white clouds. Just like a living creature drawing breath, exhaling and inhaling, the bloomers appear to have a life of their own.

The day is set fair. It's turning out just as that weatherman predicted. Not that you needed to be a genius to figure that out. But no, let's not be thinking of him again. Besides, he gets it wrong as often as he gets it right. This last thought unsettles her.

"Better put some extra pegs on just in case they get any silly ideas."

Well, being French, Mrs Mulroony's bloomers might not be 100% reliable. In fact, considering where they came from, you'd expect them to be a bit flighty, wouldn't you? Flighty. That's the key word that should have triggered the alarm. But by the time it reaches her brain, Mrs Mulroony has nodded off.

As if waiting for that very moment the lines on the weather map start getting up to all manner of mischief. The neat rows of isobars spaced out at nice regular intervals as calm as the strands on a spider's web suddenly go berserk. Like harp strings being twinged and twanged at random by unseen impish spirits, they stir up pockets of turbulence. Immediately the effects are felt in Walthamstow, where stiff gusts of wind swirl and eddy, tugging at Mrs Mulroony's French knickers with all the strength of real fingers of flesh and bone.

It isn't long before the first clothes peg has been popped. After that it's a doddle to pop the rest. Now the alarm does finally sound in Mrs Mulroony's sleepy brain. Her eyelids flutter open slowly but only just in time to see her precious white silk French knickers take off and fly away as if to join the puffy clouds scudding across the sky in a mad dance.

"Lord love a duck! What the flaming heck! This can't be true. Please tell me I'm dreaming."

But she isn't.

The scene shifts to the rooftop penthouse suite of an outrageously swanky hotel on Park Lane overlooking the lush green acres of Hyde Park. Its occupant is the world famous Italian tenor Signore Mangiatutto who is in London for a special charity concert at the Royal Albert Hall. It will be the pinnacle of an illustrious singing career. Tonight's gala performance will be broadcast to a global audience of millions. So the singer should be in the best of moods. But there is a ripple on his otherwise serene pond. He has a small problem to solve.

Through some inexplicable oversight Signore Mangiatutto has packed only one pair of his favourite XXXXXL boxer shorts made to measure by a maestro of underpants in an obscure shop tucked away in the back streets of his hometown of Naples. But what makes them really special is their cute design of blue and yellow stripes with pink polka dots. He has always worn underpants like this since he belted out his first aria at *La Scala* opera house in Milan and set off on the high road to international stardom.

Being more than a trifle superstitious, Signore Mangiatutto still ascribes his sensational overnight success to the good luck charm of these colourful bloomers that his dearest *Mamma* had made for him to mark the occasion of his debut. After that he would not dare sing without them and he's worn a succession of identical pairs of underpants in concert halls and opera houses around the world.

So under his sober black tuxedo or sumptuous operatic costume, and completely unknown to his countless fans, the large bottom of the great singer is invariably clothed in freshly laundered boxer shorts of blue and yellow stripes with pink polka dots. What would people think if they ever found out?

But right now he is more concerned what to do about having only one pair and these being in sore need of a wash. His mind is made up when he hears the TV weatherman giving the forecast.

"A very nice, bright, sunny day in prospect. Any remaining pockets of rain and cloud already clearing from the west. This will be followed by oodles of sunshine and a gentle south-westerly pussyfooting in off the Atlantic, nothing too strong, mind you, just a nice breeze to take the edge off the heat."

Oodles? Noodles? It makes him think of a bowl of *spaghetti*. No, probably more like *tagliatelli*. As for pussyfooting, he has no idea what that is supposed to mean. Something to do with kittens?

"In fact, it looks like a perfect day for hanging out the washing, ladies."

An idea begins to form in his head. So why not gentlemen too? Signore Mangiatutto has never in his whole life attempted to wash so much as a pocket handkerchief. But now, given the urgency of the situation, he resolves to take the plunge.

"That's it! I'll wash them myself."

With a quick glance up to the sunny sky he figures his underpants will easily be dry in time for this evening's performance.

As if he has a whole family's dirty clothes to deal with, Signore Mangiatutto now fills the bath with hot water. Then he empties all the colourful little bottles of shampoo and bubble bath into the rising waters. The hotel bathroom rapidly fills with soapy suds. Signore Mangiatutto is soon so wet he reckons he might as well jump in the bath and have a good soak while washing his boxer shorts at the same time.

It's such fun he can't think why he hasn't tried this before. Overflowing with happiness, he breaks into song. It's not one of those popular classical arias he's been rehearsing. To his surprise Signore Mangiatutto finds himself humming then singing an old melody once sung by Neapolitan washerwomen that he dimly remembers from his childhood in Naples.

At first he is not quite sure of the words or tune but then he falls right into the groove and it all comes flooding back. He is a little boy once more clutching at the apron strings of his jolly giant of a mother who was always either cooking or washing while his father worked long hours on the famous funicular.

He recalls his mother singing this song and how it always dried the tears and brought back a smile to his face whenever he felt sad or upset. Signore Mangiatutto is deeply moved by these childhood memories. He has come a very long way since those tough early days.

Washing his underwear is bringing unexpected rewards. He thinks he will add this forgotten song to his repertoire. Furthermore, he will dedicate tonight's gala concert to *Mamma*. That should show them he remains a man of the people, proud of his family's humble roots in the mean streets of Naples.

"Sì! Sì! Sì!"

A good half hour passes until he finally emerges from the bath. Now he showers himself and rinses his boxer shorts in cold water. Signore Mangiatutto is so buoyed up by all this happiness he is walking on air. This is no mean feat for a man of his size whose body stretches the hotel bathrobe to the limits.

There remains only the problem of how to dry his wet boxer shorts. He quickly thinks of a clever solution. He drapes them over a plastic garden chair on the balcony patio. Then he wonders whether he should fasten them somehow and goes back into the bathroom in search of whatever he might find. Soon he reappears with some safety pins and a length of dental floss.

But soon is not nearly soon enough. For Signore Mangiatutto returns to see his precious boxer shorts rise up on the wind, then hover for a few tantalising seconds above his head just out of reach. He tries to leap up and grab them like a basketball player. But try as he might, his feet don't leave the ground. He looks on powerless as his blue and yellow striped boxer shorts with pink polka dots drift ever further away rising high above his head and vanishing behind the hotel.

As they pass out of sight, something stirs deep down inside Signore Mangiatutto. Suddenly he is drowning in sadness. Then the floodgates open. So many times he has sung tragic opera on the stage, even conjuring up for the benefit of his audiences mock tears that left dramatic streaks in his make up.

But these tears are for real and there is no end to them. Cascades of warm salty water gush from his eyes and down his face into the towelling of the bath robe. In fact, the garment might have been designed for crying in, so efficiently does it soak up the tears.

Many raw emotions lurk behind all this. It's not just the loss of the boxer shorts. Poignant memories of darling *Mamma* have been awakened by that long forgotten song of the Neapolitan washerwomen. His mother had died very soon after his triumphant debut and of course no one could ever replace her.

In his grief and against the advice of his dying *Mamma* he had married a beautiful young singer from the chorus. But his new wife was only in it for his fame and fortune. She had no love for Signore Mangiatutto.

After not even a year of marriage the faithless Signora Mangiatutto sailed off into the sunset with a common or garden *gondoliere*, leaving Signore Mangiatutto to sing his heart out at the famous *La Fenice* opera house in Venice. Well, at least he received rave reviews for the evidently genuine feeling he put into his role on the night his wife walked out on him.

Today's situation is equally painful. He has come within seconds from all-time high to rock-bottom low.

Immediately he knows he is too distressed to sing at tonight's concert in the Royal Albert Hall. With that realisation comes a bout of panic. He has never before had to let his public down. He groans under his own bodyweight of sadness. To make matters worse, there is no one with whom to share his sorrows. His loneliness hits him hard and straight like a punch in the gut.

Meanwhile, over in Walthamstow, things are not looking much better for Mrs Mulroony. With her pride-and-joy super size French bloomers still flapping about in the breeze above her garden like some demented seagull there remains a dim ray of hope. They might change their mind and make a safe landing nearby where she can retrieve them. But now as they rise higher and higher drifting further and further away, that little ray of hope becomes tinier and tinier until it is completely snuffed out.

Eventually it dawns on her that she has lost them for good. Even if she did get them back, heaven knows what state they would be in. So now the party is finally over for Mrs Mulroony. She slumps back into her armchair that no longer feels half as comfy as before. She starts to pour out her sadness in words as if there is someone there to listen to her. But she lives all alone, apart from her deaf budgerigar who has given up telling himself what a pretty boy he is because he can no longer hear himself chirp.

Many years ago she kicked out that philandering, two-timing, good-for-nothing, general time-and-space-waster that was Mr Mulroony. After that life got better, but Mrs Mulroony hadn't planned to end up like this, all on her own. Now she questions whether she might have been a bit hard on Mr Mulroony? At this particular moment she could use a human ear, however useless its owner, to listen to her troubles.

Men, she reflects, hell with them, hell without them. Suddenly she feels quite sorry for herself as if her whole world has collapsed on top of her head. She sobs quietly for a few moments. Silent tears roll down her face. Then, unable to control herself a moment longer, she gives full vent to her grief. She is crying like a baby with the lungs of a giant. Even the deaf budgerigar notices something is up.

After a few minutes her tears subside. She wanders out into the garden to examine the scene of the crime. For there is no doubt in her mind that her precious French bloomers have been stolen. People nick anything nowadays, so why not undies? They'd steal the laces out of your shoes if you didn't keep your eyes peeled. So this was no freak accident but a wanton act of theft, presumably by some local villain who conjured up that rogue wind.

Who to blame? She looks accusingly at the sky, the innocent blue vacant space into which her precious confection of frilly white silk has vanished without a trace. Her suspicions linger on the weatherman whose forecast had lulled her into a false sense of security.

"If I ever catch him opening another silly supermarket, I'll have his guts for garters. Make him eat that know-all grin of his."

But what possible motive could a weatherman have for tricking her?

Mrs Mulroony stares into the empty sky. Her common sense tells her it isn't remotely logical to call the weather mischievous, moody, or capricious. But she can find no other words to describe the bizarre events taking place above her head. The clouds which should be making an orderly progress in one direction seem undecided which way to go and are scudding about hither and thither. They look like newborn lambs that don't know their woolly heads from their woolly tails.

Borne aloft on the swirling gusts and eddies Mrs Mulroony's generously proportioned French bloomers acquire a life of their own, like a great bird flapping in the breeze. One moment they are an eagle soaring, the next they turn into a gannet folding its wings to drop down and pluck a fish from the sea. Then they are snatched up by the wind, and off they go again.

All this is happening out of Mrs Mulroony's sight since the bloomers have travelled a few miles from Walthamstow in a south-westerly direction and are now approaching the office skyscrapers of the financial district known as the City of London.

The first person to see Mrs Mulroony's quite-a-bit-larger-than-average French bloomers is a very tired financial trader. He has been up half the night working the markets in the Far East. He now looks up red-eyed from his computer to take a break from the constant stream of buy-and-sell figures flashing across the screen in front of him. Not knowing much about birds but enough to know this isn't one, he immediately thinks something dangerous is about to crash into the building. He freezes, expecting an awful explosion on impact.

But nothing happens. The flying object turns out to be a piece of white cloth that he now identifies as the largest pair of knickers he has ever seen. He is about to make a joke and share it with his fellow workers but they are all glued to their screens. Then he remembers what he is meant to be doing.

Oh my god! He realises in a flash he has been pressing the short cut button *BUY NOW AT ANY PRICE I'LL TAKE THE LOT AND PAY IN CASH* for several long seconds. Now he really panics. He fears he might easily have bought the entire contents of the Tokyo Stock Exchange. Perhaps Hong Kong too? The financial trader rushes to the window and presses his face against the glass as if he could somehow escape the consequences of his massive slip up.

His sudden appearance, looking more like a mad ghost than a normal man, scares the wits out of a window cleaner precariously perched in one of those cradles suspended on ropes with a large squeegee in one hand. The shock causes him to lose his balance. He sways to and fro with agonising slowness. Then over he goes. Stupidly he has neglected to attach his safety harness. In a flash he knows he will not survive the fall onto hard concrete from 27 storeys high.

"Aaaaaaaaaaaaaaaaaaaaarrrgh!!!!!!!!!!!!!!!!!!!!!"

Defying death, a desperate never-say-die instinct prompts him to flail about with both arms as if there might be a stray rope end to catch hold of. But there isn't. It's something else that he latches on to. By some miracle his clutching fingers grasp the edges of Mrs Mulroony's extremely voluminous French knickers.

The window cleaner holds on tight. He has a life line. Now he is no longer falling quite so fast. With the aid of this improvised parachute he descends gently to the ground. And to make matters better he manages to land on a small soft patch of lawn that cushions his fall. Against all the odds he is saved, alive and well, after a free fall from the 27th floor!

His first thought is to buy a drink for his mates and tell them all about it. Then they'll want to buy him one just to hear his story all over again. He'll have free beers for life on the strength of it. But what if they don't believe him? No problem, he'll show them the evidence. But in the excitement of his narrow escape the window cleaner released his grip on Mrs Mulroony's outrageously oversize French bloomers.

He makes a quick search around him but finds nothing. Though when he looks up to measure the distance of his fall from the empty cradle suspended 27 storeys high he spots his heaven sent parachute in the unlikely shape of a gigantic pair of French knickers being carried away on the wind.

At the same moment, Signore Mangiatutto's XXXXXL boxer shorts are drifting this way and that in the turbulent breeze over Mayfair. This posh, expensive district full of diplomatic missions and opulent mansions lies immediately behind the hotel on Park Lane where they had broken free just a few moments earlier. Now they flap lazily towards Grosvenor Square which this morning is the scene of some rather frantic activity.

A small crowd is gathered in front of the concrete and steel barricades recently put up to protect the great palace of the American Embassy from its enemies. Judging from all the cars, cameras, cables, vans with satellite dishes and an empty speaker's lectern bristling with microphones it is clear that a big media event is about to get rolling.

A gaggle of hyper-active people with clipboards flap about excitedly looking at their watches every two seconds. All eyes are fixed on the grand staircase of the American Embassy waiting for the glass doors to open. So no-one notices Signore Mangiatutto's colourful underwear hovering over the scene.

Suspense mounts as the minutes tick away. The buzz of anticipation gets louder and louder. Then suddenly everyone is silent for no particular reason. At this precise moment the doors open and a posse of security men in dark suits and dark glasses march forth. As yet it's impossible to say who is the star attraction. Speculation is rife among the press corps.

"Can't be the Pres. He's meant to be giving a speech at the UN in New York in a couple of hours."

"Anyway, not his style to meet the media if he can get someone else to do it."

"Surely he wouldn't send the Vice?"

"Not unless he wants to have a laugh."

A huge groan of disappointment goes up when a portly silver haired man in a dull grey suit steps forward waving a sheaf of papers.

"It's only the Ambassador."

"Can't be that important then."

"So why do they have to summon us here?"

"Surely a press release would do the business?"

But here they all are so they might as well listen to what he has to say.

"Ladies and gentleman of the British press. Fellow defenders of freedom. We have stood shoulder to shoulder through good times and bad. Now more than ever we need to know who our friends are in an increasingly dangerous world."

All this is going out live to TV and radio networks around the world. The Ambassador knows he will probably never have an audience like this again. He has been up half the night with a team of speech writers working on every single word. But he has added some rather neat touches of his own which he hopes will hit just the right note and generally give some lustre to his uneventful career in public life.

"Standing before you all here today in front of this fine building, a solid sign of our firm commitment to the United Kingdom and …"

This is the cue for the cameras to move away from the Ambassador and pan steadily across the façade of the American Embassy.

"… fluttering overhead the star spangled banner, proud symbol of our nation's cherished hopes …"

Now the TV cameras track slowly up the pole until they reach the flag and zoom in like marksmen taking aim. At this point the Ambassador makes a dramatic pause. Having created a suitably serious mood he is ready to move on to the matter in hand. It's all going perfectly to plan. His political masters back in Washington DC will be impressed.

But as he looks up from his script, instead of grave expressions he sees rows of smiling faces not directed at him but at something above his head. Then, to his horror a great roar of laughter goes up. And he hasn't even tried to crack a joke yet. Realising he has lost his audience, the Ambassador turns and looks up to see the cause of their merriment.

Instead of the red white and blue of the Stars and Stripes it's the blue and yellow stripes with pink polka dots of Signore Mangiatutto's XXXXXL boxer shorts that have pride of place on the flagpole draped over the American flag and hiding it from view.

Knowing full well that these images are being broadcast live to the big wide world, the Ambassador tries to figure out how to get attention away from that ridiculous thing whatever it is and back to his speech. Now the mobile phone in his pocket starts to ring.

Amplified through the many loudspeakers the ringing fills Grosvenor Square. The TV cameras refocus their lenses on him. Once again he has the full attention of his audience though he dearly wishes he hadn't.

Normally under such circumstances, he would make a muttered apology and switch off the phone before resuming his speech. But this phone is different. It's his personal hot line to the White House. Not to answer the President's call would be quite unthinkable. Perhaps a treasonable offence? Still it feels completely wrong to be taking the call in front of the world's media hooked up on live feeds to here, there and everywhere.

Shaking with nerves, he answers the phone.

"Yes, Mr President?"

The Ambassador tries to sound business-like and confident but he trembles at the President's voice.

"What the hell do think you are up to? Making a mockery of our nation's flag?"

At the mention of flag the cameras refocus on the blue and yellow stripes with pink polka dots of Signore Mangiatutto's XXXXXL boxer shorts still fluttering gaily for all to see from the flagpole of the American Embassy. Meanwhile, the microphones pick up every word of the presidential ticking off.

"You're fired! With immediate effect. I hereby order you, Mr ex-Ambassador, under the legal powers vested in me, to get your stupid fat arse out of there tootie sweet. Surrender your diplomatic passport to Security. You're under arrest for... for... Well, I'll think of something. Make no mistake about that."

The line goes dead. Mr ex-Ambassador can do no more than fold the pages of his undelivered speech and bow humbly to the crowd.

"That's all folks. Thank you and goodbye."

This really gets the press buzzing. At news desks around the world front pages are being hastily rewritten. No one stops to ask themselves what the great speech would have been about. Everyone is so gripped by the spectacle of the diplomat being escorted back inside the building by his own security staff.

A newsman now trains his camera on the flag that sparked off this diplomatic incident. But Signore Mangiatutto's XXXXXL boxer shorts have been carried away on yet another gust of wind while no one was looking. Once again the star spangled banner flies high in proud and glorious isolation. The question now rippling across everyone's lips is what country or maybe liberation movement did that exotic flag represent?

But the one person who can enlighten them is totally unaware of what has been happening. Signore Mangiatutto is sitting in a darkened hotel room with the TV set switched off wondering how on earth he is going to sing this evening at the Royal Albert Hall without his special lucky underpants.

As if seeking to upstage Signore Mangiatutto's XXXXXL boxer shorts, Mrs Mulroony's ample French knickers now steal the limelight in equally spectacular fashion. After saving the life of a window cleaner in the City they come scudding across town on a stiff easterly breeze. Suddenly the wind drops and they swoop down like a bird of prey towards Buckingham Palace where thousands of tourists are gathered for the Changing of the Guard.

With all eyes on the spectacular parade of troops in red tunics and black bearskin hats no-one sees what's coming until it's actually happened. One moment everything is perfectly normal with the band playing and people taking pictures. And the next, the soldier leading the procession has an enormous white flag fluttering from the sharp bayonet fixed on the barrel of his rifle. But he doesn't appear to notice it since his rigid gaze is trained straight ahead with traditional military discipline.

One person who does notice is a distinguished silver-haired gent lounging about on the first floor balcony of Buckingham Palace. He is enjoying the first sip of a martini cocktail after a late breakfast and all is right with the world. He doesn't usually watch the Changing of the Guard. The routine has become rather stale through repetition over the years.

But today it feels different and he follows proceedings with renewed interest. It takes a moment or two for the penny to drop, but when it does the grey hairs on his neck bristle in an alarming manner. He rushes back inside the palace, scarcely able to describe what he has seen to the elderly lady seated at the breakfast table studying the form in the Racing Post for the 2.30 at Sandown Park.

"Egad, Lizzie! You'll never believe this, old girl. It's the Guard … the Changing of the … I mean the new lot taking over … well they're carrying a flag … a big, white flag … looks like we've surrendered … I think I need another drink."

Only now does the lady look up from her paper.

"Surrendered, Philip? To whom, may I ask, has one surrendered?"

"How should I know? Surrender is surrender. So does it matter? It's all over, Lizzie. The game's up."

"You're not making any sense, Philip. I told you it was too early for that cocktail."

"This is no joke, Lizzie. If you don't believe me, come and see for yourself."

The lady walks over to the window in a stately, regal sort of way and surveys the scene from behind a curtain. Her silence confirms the unlikely truth of what her husband has told her. Finally she speaks.

"I expect it's one of Charles's new-fangled ideas. We did agree he could modernise certain aspects of court ceremonial, didn't we?"

"Charlie boy? Dammit! Our very own Carlos the Jackal! Who else? The POW must be behind this. Just typical of his modern madcap schemes. But how could he surrender just like that? Surely the Windsors are made of sterner stuff?"

Lizzie has seen Philip in similar fighting mood many times before, but never quite as fired up as this. So she bides her time, biting her lip.

"Come on, Lizzie. I'm assuming command. No time to lose. Get your skates on. We can slip out the back. Fly the chopper to Sandringham. Lie low for a few days in one of those cottages, get some false passports, book a cheap flight from Stansted. Leave it all to me. I still own a Greek island. Kept that up my sleeve. Thought it might come in handy. Nice little bolt hole for an emergency just like this. Didn't think we'd ever have to use it though."

While Philip and Lizzie make their escape plans, the Racing Post lies discarded on the breakfast table. As it turns out, Lizzie has picked the winner of the 2.30 at Sandown Park, a rank outsider at 33-1. But in the heat of the moment she omits to phone her bookie.

Later, when they realise the surrender was a hoax, and for once nothing to do with Charles, Lizzie has some sharp words for Philip that leave him sulking in the scullery over a few more stiff martinis.

Meanwhile, Mrs Mulroony's larger-than-life French bloomers have freed themselves from the soldier's bayonet and are off on their travels again zipping along at high speed over the wide open spaces of Hyde Park. Briefly, they catch on the mast of a model sailing boat on the Round Pond in Kensington Gardens. Immediately, the yacht surges forward at a healthy rate of knots, rapidly overhauling all the noisy radio-controlled motorboats.

"That's cheating, Fotherington-Thomas. You've got an illegal spinnaker."

But the proud schoolboy owner of the ship smiles smugly at his rivals.

"Get your smelly boats out of my way. Sail has priority over power. That's the rule of the sea."

Signore Mangiatutto's colourful XXXXXL boxer shorts are also turning heads. An ornithologist mistakes them for a rare tropical specimen from South America and phones the bird watchers' hotline. Within minutes twitchers all over London drop whatever they are doing and rush to the scene of the reported sighting. Media attention also follows the exploits of Mrs Mulroony's horrendously huge French knickers as they are blown to and fro across London.

Each set of underwear has its own followers in hot pursuit. They collide with one another in Trafalgar Square when for a few seconds the boxer shorts and French knickers swirl in an aerial dance around the head of Admiral Nelson on the top of his column.

The press has a field day chasing down silly stories. The papers can hardly keep up with the fast breaking news. There have never been so many items to make the front page in a single day. The number of banner headlines to appear breaks all previous records.

MAN SAVED BY MIRACLE PARACHUTE

WINDOW CLEANER CHEATS DEATH

COUP ATTEMPT AT US EMBASSY

TOP ENVOY FIRED

WHITE FLAG SCARE FOR WINDSORS

PALACE SURRENDER HOAX

MASSIVE HUNT FOR RARE BIRDS

UFOS OVER LONDON

PM TO ADDRESS NATION

An undercover reporter posing as a footman in Buckingham Palace overhears Lizzie and Philip's hastily hatched escape plans to that Greek island. His amazing story merits an equally amazing headline:

ROYAL KNICKERS IN A TWIST

This comes closest to the honest truth behind the strange events that have not only Londoners but people all over the world on the edge of their seats. But speaking the words 'royal' and 'knickers' in one breath is judged a tad disrespectful to Her Britannic Majesty and so the headline goes unpublished.

Oblivious to all the fuss and bother sparked off by the antics of their respective undergarments Mrs Mulroony and Signore Mangiatutto remain in blissful ignorance of the uproar they have unwittingly caused. But blissful is hardly the word to describe the mood of these two sad individuals, each bowed down under the enormous weight of private misery that is simply too much to bear.

Over in Walthamstow Mrs Mulroony has been slumped in her armchair all day long quite unable to move a muscle. The hour for lunch has come and gone completely unremarked. The flowery bone china cup and saucer she prefers for afternoon tea stay untouched in the dresser. It is now approaching 5pm.

Any moment now there will be a knock on the door of Signore Mangiatutto's hotel room in Park Lane to wake him after his usual deep siesta following the generous luncheon he needs to fuel his powerful singing voice. But he has had nothing to eat all day. For once his appetite has let him down. Nor has he had a wink of sleep He knows his concert will be a disaster. He will have to cry off sick if he is not to disgrace himself and destroy a lifetime's reputation.

Signore Mangiatutto thinks of all the many people getting ready for tonight's gala concert at the Royal Albert Hall: musicians putting on their formal evening dress and polishing instruments of wood and brass, the ushers and programme sellers, stage hands and technicians who will soon be heading for bus stops and tube stations. He thinks also of the thousands of concert goers already taking an early dinner before the show. It is too much to contemplate.

But then Signore Mangiatutto thinks of the millions of TV viewers around the world he is about to disappoint. This should be the final straw to break the camel's back and finish him off. But it has the opposite effect on the celebrity tenor. It is a rallying call. As if to lift the weight of the world bearing down on his shoulders, he rises from his chair in a last attempt to regain control over his destiny.

Even as Signore Mangiatutto gets unsteadily to his feet, he feels dizzy. He can't sing in this condition. It is hopeless. He totters over to the glass patio door and looks out. A dark thought crosses his mind. Why not end it all? The parapet wall is low enough for him to haul himself over. Then the seven storey drop from his balcony should do the business.

But he pauses to consider what a revolting sight he will make splattered all over the pavement dressed only in a hotel bathrobe that doesn't even fit him properly. So Signore Mangiatutto shakes his head and wearily turns away. In that moment he catches sight of something unusual out of the corner of his eye.

Draped over the back of the plastic chair is a huge pair of white silk knickers. He can't believe his eyes. What kind of woman could these belong to? The answer of course is to a very big lady. That much is immediately obvious to Signore Mangiatutto. But his speculations on the identity of the mystery owner are quickly overtaken by another thought. Or rather it's not so much a thought as an impulse.

He is seized by a sudden urge to slip into the French knickers. The naughtiness of wearing ladies underwear is irresistible in itself. It's a common enough fantasy that for all he knows may have been stalking him since childhood. But Signore Mangiatutto is now driven by something altogether more powerful than a playful whim. An instinct he can barely describe let alone comprehend has taken hold and will not let him go. It's a life-changing moment.

Reverential as a priest Signore Mangiatutto carries the French knickers into his hotel room, admiring the frilly bits stitched along the edges of the fine white silk. Then he inspects them inside and out. The only identification is a small label with the words *MADE IN FRANCE* in capital letters.

Made in France? That sounds exciting. Drawing breath and trembling with emotion he discards the bathrobe, stands for a moment in front of a full length mirror naked as the day he was born. Then he closes his eyes and in a single swift movement, surprisingly graceful for a man of his great girth, he bends down, steps daintily into the French knickers and pulls them up around his waist.

Immediately, he tingles with excitement. Life pulses through his veins with a prickling sensation. It's like he has been born again. Now Signore Mangiatutto opens his eyes and looks at himself in the mirror.

Dio mio! What a perfect picture! What a fine figure he cuts! He is delighted by the transformation in his appearance. Not only does he look brilliant, he feels brilliant too. The French knickers fit him to perfection. Not a tight spot anywhere, pleasantly cool against his flesh and so light they might have been made of air. Overcome with ecstasy, and all his problems forgotten, he bursts spontaneously into song.

Only after he has finished does he recognise the melody. It's another old Neapolitan song, this one a lullaby *Mamma* always sang when he couldn't sleep. He hasn't heard it since he was a child but now there it is in his throat and on his lips in all its wonder and glory. It's as if dear old *Mamma* is right there with him now stroking his hair, telling him everything is OK and all his problems will be taken care of.

Indeed, Signore Mangiatutto now feels without a care in the world. All the fear and anxiety about not being able to sing at his gala concert this evening has vanished. He pirouettes on his toes and dances around the room still naked but for the frilly French knickers. He knows his performance will be the crowning point of a glittering career. Tonight he will sing like he has never sung before. His fans will go wild. And all thanks to this mysterious pair of French bloomers. Life is indeed a wonderful thing.

Half an hour later when Signore Mangiatutto hears a knock on the door, there he is ready already, resplendent in his shiny black evening suit, a healthy rose pink tint to his complexion and a saucy twinkle in his eye. His personal assistant, a serious young lady with the starchy manner of a Victorian nanny notices he is looking rather pleased with himself.

"Good to see you looking so exceedingly well, Signore Mangiatutto."

But all she gets is the enigmatic reply.

"Vive la France!"

"France, Signore Mangiatutto? But surely the Paris concert is next week. Tonight it's London. That's London, as in London, England."

"London, Vienna, Milan, New York. For me it will always be France wherever I am."

"Very well, Signore Mangiatutto. *Vive la France!* Just as you say."

The idea is forming in Signore Mangiatutto's head that these magical French knickers will now take the place of his lucky boxer shorts. For that reason he will always be in debt to France.

If the real owner of the French knickers were to know how happy they have made the celebrated Italian singer, would that make her feel any better? It's hard to say. Mrs Mulroony is so sad you might imagine a dark cloud hanging right over her tiny house in Walthamstow. She sits motionless in her armchair absolutely numb with gloom. She stares straight ahead at her three china ducks nailed in mid flight to the living room wall. She reckons she knows exactly how they must feel. She can't take her eyes off them.

The outside world no longer exists for her. So she doesn't see the colourful item of gentleman's underwear come floating down out of the sky to end up hanging neatly draped over the washing line between the apple tree and garden shed.

But then the extra loud cawing of a crow makes Mrs Mulroony turn her head just a fraction to check what's going on. Can't have that greedy beggar eating her apples, now can she? Of course not. And in that instant something odd catches her eye.

"What the Dickens!"

Before she knows it she is out of the armchair and on her feet. Mrs Mulroony hasn't stirred her stumps all day but now she hurries over to the French window and looks out. There, hanging from the washing line in exactly the same place as were her precious French knickers that went west with the wind many hours ago is an exotic garment the likes of which she has never seen before.

The louder than life blue and yellow stripes and pink polka dots of Signore Mangiatutto's XXXXXL boxer shorts are so bright and garish they are painful to behold. For Mrs Mulroony generally prefers the softer pastel shades on the colour chart: a nice magnolia, a peach blossom or a hint of lavender. Instinctively, she averts her gaze. Then she looks again and finds herself drawn to the dazzling hues and striking pattern which excite her imagination while causing her to tremble with uncertainty. It's like a London pigeon seeing a tropical parrot for the first time.

Mrs Mulroony now contemplates the garment with the eye of an art lover at the Royal Academy. The combination of pink, yellow and blue could be from the palette of one of those famous painters. She can't remember his name. French chappie most likely.

This thought brings to mind her sadly mourned frilly French knickers that had been hanging from the very same washing line only this morning. Now she makes some kind of hazy connection between her missing underwear and this alien visitor which she now recognises as a pair of gentleman's XXXXXL boxer shorts. That's more than a coincidence, surely?

Then she has another thought. Just suppose another gust of wind were to carry off these boxer shorts just like what happened to her fancy French knickers. Golly! They're not even pegged down!

Purposefully, she hurries out into the garden, grabbing a large wicker basket on the way, strides over to the washing line, takes down the boxer shorts and folds them carefully into the basket. Her expert fingers immediately detect finely spun cotton of the highest quality. Nothing like silk, mind you, but ever so light and pleasantly cool to the touch.

She carries her prize back inside the house. But Mrs Mulroony is unsure where to put them. She can't place the gents boxer shorts in a drawer next to her own smalls. Or should that be bigs? She smiles at her own joke, then checks herself. No, that would hardly be proper and decent. Though to tell the truth she doesn't want to put them away at all.

So she drapes them over the empty armchair once occupied by Mr Mulroony. The blue and yellow stripes and pink polka dots of Signore Mangiatutto's XXXXXL boxer shorts don't exactly go with Mrs Mulroony's décor, but they do bring warmth and a dash of excitement to her living room. It's like having some colourful character on a visit keeping you company.

They have such a presence she almost wants to talk to them. She stops herself just in time from doing anything so daft, then falls to wondering who might be the owner. But idle speculation sits awkwardly with a sensible woman like Mrs Mulroony.

Don't go sticking your nose into what doesn't concern you. That's her motto. Though she can't resist a quick sniff of the boxer shorts and is delighted to note they are freshly laundered and nicely aired and giving off the scent of a variety of expensive toiletries rather than some common detergent.

As you may have gathered, Mrs Mulroony is feeling loads better than before. Not that she has forgotten the tragic loss of her frilly French knickers, though the arrival of the boxer shorts has cheered her up considerably. Her healthy appetite now returns to remind her she has missed out on lunch and afternoon tea. So she takes a fish pie out of the freezer and pops it in the microwave. Before she hits the start button she opens a packet of salt and vinegar crisps and pours herself a large glass of sweet sherry.

The first sip hits her empty stomach with a warm surge that spreads throughout her whole body. Life doesn't seem so bad after all. For good measure she pours herself a second glass of sherry while licking the last crumbs of the salt and vinegar crisps from her sticky fingers. Now she feels quite tiddly and decides it's time for the fish pie. It tastes delicious and she gobbles it down in record time at the kitchen table.

Afterwards she settles back in her comfy armchair and digs the remote control from its usual hiding place under the cushion. At the third click she succeeds in turning on the TV. As the screen flickers into life it shows the animated evening scene outside the Royal Albert Hall. Crowds of excited people are arriving for the concert. A big banner announces the star turn to be the great Italian tenor, the one and only maestro of music: Signore Mangiatutto.

Now some people might call his singing style a bit sentimental, even sugary along the edges, but Mrs Mulroony is not alone in thinking he is the honey on the almonds, the tomato sauce on the pasta, the chocolate powder on the cappuccino. Why, the sweet feeling he brings to those heart-breaking arias is enough to draw tears from the eyes of a sphinx.

Mrs Mulroony turns up the volume and wiggles her buttocks deeper into the soft cushion. There will be time enough tomorrow to dwell on her missing French knickers but this evening she's not going to let that spoil her enjoyment of Signore Mangiatutto's gala performance.

And what a concert it is! The TV cameras show Signore Mangiatutto strutting his stuff on the stage with all the *braggadocio* of a circus ringmaster or flamenco dancer. Shoulders thrust back, chest puffed out, his voice carries loud and clear to the distant seats at the top of the gallery.

Signore Mangiatutto has hardly got going but it's clear he's on top of his game. He has found a little bit extra, that mysterious certain something which sends a tingle up the spine, a magic ingredient so special not even the singer can explain let alone control it. Signore Mangiatutto is on song, quite literally on song. His gala performance is an absolutely ripping triumph.

When it comes to an encore Signore Mangiatutto decides to give it all he's got. He takes the deepest breath he has ever drawn in his long singing career and lets himself go. He holds nothing back. He follows the inspiration of the moment wherever it might lead him, unthinking and without question.

Tonight his voice feels massive, daring him to go further than he has ever gone before. He drops down as far as is humanly possible, then finds he can descend another note or two. Then he comes up for air and soars to the top of the musical scale. The tenor's voice goes higher and higher, becoming an alto then a treble, after that a soprano, and then castrato. Finally Signore Mangiatutto breaks free from vocal limits like a rocket launched into space. Now he is in orbit.

Glass chandeliers are tinkling. Still his voice goes higher. His lungs, strong as bellows, cannot give much more. They strain to deliver their last ounce of breath while his stomach swells and swells under the effort.

Suddenly he has gone too far. He is over the top, past the point of no return. His face is as purple as the satin cummerbund around his waist which now gives way under the strain and bursts. Waistcoat buttons pop open. His trousers explode and collapse into a heap at his ankles. And there for everyone to see under the cold eye of the TV cameras is the alarming sight of the world famous tenor wearing a pair of white silk French knickers with frilly bits along the edges.

Like a true professional, Signore Mangiatutto finishes his song with his trousers down, not caring how ridiculous he looks. Then he takes his bow sheltering behind an enormous bouquet of flowers. His face flushed with success he thanks his fans a hundred times and finally exits to his dressing room.

The astonishment reverberating around the Royal Albert Hall is nothing compared to that of Mrs Mulroony in her little house in Walthamstow. She can hardly believe what she's seen. There was her favourite singer standing bold as brass on the stage of the Royal Albert Hall wearing her precious French bloomers.

Her emotions are all mixed up. She has been moved by every single note of Signore Mangiatutto's sensational singing. At one point she wanted to reach out and kiss him. But then to cap it all, seeing him wearing her lost French knickers!

Words can't begin to describe the turmoil inside her head. Breathless and open mouthed, Mrs Mulroony watches the TV, unable to tear herself away. Now the cameras are going backstage. She sees the name of Signore Mangiatutto on a dressing room door. There is going to be an interview. She gapes spellbound while the great tenor modestly accepts the plaudits.

The interviewer is far too polite to enquire about the French knickers. But Signore Mangiatutto, when asked to explain the secret of his amazing performance, comes straight to the point. He describes his total despair that morning at losing his favourite XXXXXL boxer shorts, though he omits to mention their exotic blue and yellow stripes with pink polka dots.

Mrs Mulroony looks long and hard at the item of gentleman's underwear still draped over the back of the former Mr Mulroony's armchair. Meanwhile, she listens to Signore Mangiatutto tell how the mysterious pair of French bloomers came to the rescue in the very nick of time. As if sent from heaven they were and he can only give full credit to the French knickers and indeed to the entire French nation for his amazing triumph tonight.

"Vive la France! Vive la France!"

Now he says something which shakes Mrs Mulroony in a way she has never been shaken before.

"I would like to thank the gracious lady who sent me her beautiful French knickers in my hour of need. Such a sensitive sacrifice. I feel for her what we Italians call *amore*. I offer her my hand in marriage."

Amore? That's a fine way to go about things, proposing to a respectable lady in public with the whole world listening in. But in spite of her misgivings, Mrs Mulroony is out of her armchair in a flash.

"Right, fatso. I'm on my way."

She scoops up Signore Mangiatutto's XXXXXL boxer shorts and heads for the front door. Minutes later she is riding a 55 bus into central London. She'll have to change to a number 10 in Oxford Street. So it looks like a long trip to the Royal Albert Hall. But that's OK. It's not ladylike to be in a hurry, is it?

Signore Mangiatutto is in for a surprise, a huge surprise as it happens. But that's just the sort of surprise he likes. He is head over heels in love with a woman he hasn't yet met. He adores everything about her on the strength of her magical underwear. She is all he ever dreamed of and more. He yearns to marry her no matter what, even without her knickers, if you see what I'm getting at. It's *amore*, the real thing. He wants to see the magic word printed in big, bold capital letters on billboards all over London:

AMORE! AMORE! AMORE!

But what the billboard writers come up with is:

ITALIAN CROONER IN

SEXY UNDIES – PICTURES!

Well, that's the British press for you, absolutely no sense of romance.

The story could end right here at this point, because the outcome must be pretty obvious, even though the actual ending has yet to happen. Mrs Mulroony's 55 bus has ground to a halt in a diabolical traffic jam in Clerkenwell. Burst water main, puddles everywhere, big mess, major diversions. She could be stuck there for hours. And then what?

But Mrs Mulroony is no pessimist. She reckons when she eventually gets to meet Signore Mangiatutto in the flesh she'll pull out his XXXXXL boxer shorts from her handbag with a great flourish. Or maybe she should put them on beforehand and twirl her skirt like a cancan dancer? Yes, that's more like it. He won't be expecting that, now will he? Already her heart thumps to the Latino beat of *amore, amore, amore.*

She's not so really sure though how she feels about Signore Mangiatutto wearing her precious French knickers. Generally, Mrs Mulroony doesn't hold with that sort of thing. On the other hand he did sing like a lark when he had them on, didn't he? Sweet enough to make the angels cry for joy. So maybe she'll think about making an exception now and then for when he does special gala concerts for charity and suchlike.

So on balance, it promises to be a good, solid relationship based on a healthy dose of mutual respect and give and take. The signs are indeed favourable that Mrs Mulroony and Signore Mangiatutto will live happily ever after. It looks like a match made in heaven.

www.ingramcontent.com/pod-product-compliance
Lightning Source LLC
Chambersburg PA
CBHW032027040426
42448CB00006B/757